# A SENSE OF VALUES

# A SENSE OF VALUES

Lewis Chase

Philosophical Library
New York

This little book is dedicated to my mother, father, wife, sister, daughters, and sons—those whom I love so much but somehow do not say so enough—

—and also to those many beautiful friends—Dick, Joan, Jane, Paul, Roland, Bernice, George, Roy, Alice, Lois, Janice, Mac, Barbara, John, Ellie, Earl, Florence, Clark, Mary, Alex, Gerald, and many others. I have watched you bear your trials and suffering and joys with awe and growing admiration for you over the years. Much of what is on these pages has been transmitted to my pen directly from you in ways you cannot know. You, collectively, are its author more than I. I am only the observer—the scribe who without original thought writes down what is seen, heard, felt, or known in the heart—without ability or desire to pass final judgement on anyone—but an observer who has infinite respect and love for all of you—

—and to hundreds of naked and malnourished and sometimes diseased children around the world, to whom over the years I have thrown a Rupee, or a Real, or a Piaster, or a Peso, and then gone to my room and stared at the ceiling for hours trying to fathom a feeling of absoulte helplessness.

—and to Erasmus

# CONTENTS

There is not an original thought on these pages. Every one is plagiarized and I admit it freely. I have simply changed the words to hide the sources—and there have been so many sources that I have forgotton which thought came from where—but perhaps the reader will not find that so bad.

---------------------------------------------------------------------------

Children, you are now mostly grown and gone
It seems but yesterday when you were born
Our love for you is infinite
There is so much to tell you from our experience
But you don't want to listen
And that may be good
For though you came from us
You are not us
You are you—and you must have your own experience
So we love you and know that you love us
Though neither you nor we say it well with our voice
But we say it with our eyes upon you
And our concerns for you
And our hopes for your well being and your treasured indi-
    viduality
You cannot understand our concerns
But you will in time with your own children or with your life's
    struggles
And when you do we will again grow close
In person or in memory—it doesn't matter
And then we will be close forever

---------------------------------------------------------------------------

# OF THE PAST, THE FUTURE, AND OF VALUES

There is a coming economic, sociological, and perhaps spiritual dislocation in our western society.

While there is a great deal that can be done to soften its blow and perhaps even turn it to certain advantages if we are very wise, there is no way to prevent it. If there is a way to delay it, even that may not be wise.

This little book is not about prophecy, or mysticism, or the coming of the end of the world, or anything like that. No great spiritual revelation is needed to see approximately what is coming.

Nor is it a call to repentance for those guilty of causing the coming events, for no one is knowingly guilty. Throughout history, in every catastrophic event, the attempt is made to identify the causative villains and punish them.

Vilification is never intellectually honest, but in the coming events it is particularly inappropriate. There are really no clear-cut villains in our future dilemma. Perhaps there have been none in many of the past catastrophies either, but those are behind us. What concerns us is what is immediately ahead.

1

If anything, this book is a plea for both spiritual and intellectual honesty (in their strictest meaning) on the part of all of us and directed at ourselves in searching out our true sense of values.

We do not do this in any sense of regressive guilt—that great Achilles heel of Christian religion—but in the sense of the way that our examination of values can help us to perhaps a somewhat less affluent but a greater and more mature (and perhaps even more miraculous) world ahead.

Why is it that the western world seems to be approaching such a sharp discontinuity with its past? That past, which stretches back through the centuries to the renaissance and beyond, has been characterized by a rising faith in the benefits yielded by the intellectual pursuit of science and philosophy, and the translation of the knowledge thereby accrued to technological and political practice. For about the last century and a half, those material benefits have burgeoned (for some of us) beyond imagination.

As we grew out of a time of dogmatic faith into the so-called Age of Reason, suffering was not absent and the turmoil was occasionally great, but many things seemed to bloom—medicine, science, technology, law, philosophy, to name a few. Monarchial governments waned and republics arose, and their economies flourished, at least for a small but dominant fraction of the earth's human population.

It seemed as though there was no reason, if we kept our rational wits about us, why we could not continue forever upward. If we but tried we might even create a better life for everyone on this earth.

True, we lapsed into occasional savage wars as we have done throughout history, but we recovered from each of them to continue the upward climb. We even idealistically fought wars to end wars, or so we thought anyway.

We created railroads, antibiotics, automobiles, computers, jet airplanes, civil rights movements, power plants, environ-

-------------------------------------------------------------------

God makes no promise of material gain
    to those who serve him in this world
No assured fame or fortune
Only sweat, disappointment, and occasionally
    a short moment of seeming success
And the satisfaction of devoting one's life to something
    worthwhile

-------------------------------------------------------------------

mental movements, sexual revolutions, and so forth, all directed "upwards" and toward "a better quality of life."

All of these things were at least partly good—all were for the most part well-intentioned even if occasionally at cross purposes.

But what did "upward" and "quality" and "better" really mean? How is it that we now must face the economic and cultural discontinuity of which we speak? Why is it not certain that "progress" will not simply continue to improve things for us as it has in the past century or two?

One illustration of the discontinuity dilemma is implicit in the history of medical science and its interaction with technology. In the last two centuries the causes of many of humanity's most debilitating diseases have been discovered and cures effected, thus increasing man's life span possibilities. The increase in life span possibilities is not synonomous with an increase in life span however. Such things as clothing, food, housing, employment, and population control are integral parts of an increased life span. In developed countries, mainly through the harnessing of fossil energy, most of these things have been provided by science and technology. New agricultural techniques teamed with modern machines driven by energy taken from holes in the ground have provided the food and fibre and released the labor force necessary to produce a life of convenience that would have been envied by the greatest of ancient kings.

In less developed countries the benefits, though great, have not always been so clear-cut. While medical science has cut infant mortality, and technology has improved food production and provided some life-improving jobs, the rapidly increasing populations often appear to be outrunning whatever other gains are being made. The Four Horsemen of the Apocalypse are never far away. Many persons who have devoted their lives to "improve" the lot of others through medi-

4

cine and technology find themselves in awe of what may be just ahead.

And this is not only true in the underdeveloped nations. Only in recent years have we undertaken a real study of how we have used our resources in agriculture, in materials, and in energy, and we are not at all sure we can sustain the material heights we have achieved. Some are not even sure we want to do so.

A second, and perhaps more frightening indication of the coming dilemma is the growing crisis in energy and material resources now spreading over all the earth. As we thrash around searching for someone (anyone will do really) to blame, we collectively cannot seem to look back at the long road that got us where we are, and thus we cannot determine the direction of the long road ahead that we must travel.

Really what has happened is quite simple. Roughly one hundred and fifty years ago, science, mathematics, and the social climate congealed in a unique and special way that allowed human beings to radically increase their rate of material progress. An enormous and powerful industrial engine was created with many facets. Like any powerful being, however, that engine had an Achilles heel that has ultimately made it extremely vulnerable. It ran on fossil fuels of finite availability, and it doubled its consumption of those fuels every ten years or so. Those fuels were so cheap that their total cost, at least up to now, has been a trivial part of the cost of building and operating the rest of the economic engine, and thus we forgot to consider them in our desire to continue expanding everything. But as every mathematician, scientist, and engineer knows, any resource for which the demand increases exponentially must eventually run out. If this exponential increase in consumption were to continue, it would mean that in the next ten years or so we would consume as much fuel as we have ever consumed in all the previous one hundred fifty years. If it were to continue for a decade after that, we would consume during that second decade twice as much fuel as in all that past history before now. In the third decade, we would consume four times as much energy as we have up to now, and so on. Clearly, such a process simply cannot keep running forever or, as it turns out, even for very much longer.

What is true for energy is equally true for many other resources which can vary from mined metals and chemicals, to plant nutrients in the soils, to oxygen-producing plant life, to many other things. We are rapidly coming to the end of a one hundred and fifty year binge which has essentially been a free ride in the developed world.

A century and a half ago, our great-great-grandparents lived not too much differently (in a material sense) from the way people had lived from time immemorial, and as much of the world still does, at least in part. We say in part because there are extremely few places on earth which have not been deeply touched by the advances of western technology in some way. Almost no one has been left completely unaffected by at least a radio, or an automobile, or a book, or a propane stove, or a steel hoe, or shovel, or some little knick-knack that is stamped *a product of one hundred fifty years of western civilization*. Really, almost no one is left alive who actually remembers how things were before. That is probably just as well, because we cannot go back to the way things were before anyway. The earth cannot sustain four billion people with methods which were used to sustain a few hundred million.

We must now chart a new course for civilization, and the adventure ahead will be as great as any in past history. We are going to change, irrespective of whether we wish to do so or not.

In part we have plundered the earth of its easily accessible resources to create material wealth for a few of us. There is

6

no point in hanging our heads in guilt. We were not wise enough to see our great mistakes. We saw only our great successes, and there were both. The earth still has adequate resources and perhaps always will if we manage things wisely, but we must now be more careful and respectful in extracting them. Ultimately (meaning in the near future) we must adopt the practice of carefully renewing the ones we extract. Fortunately it can be done, and we may even be able to preserve basic human freedoms in the process if we are collectively very wise.

There are many scientific and technical things we can and must do. However, we must also understand that the malaise creeping over the earth has even deeper roots that cannot be eliminated by scientific and technical quick fixes. We must try to understand why, with the best of intentions, we have driven civilization to the edge of a cliff. If we do not understand why, our quick fixes will only lead us to another cliff, and at some time, there will not be enough quick fixes to avoid a major human calamity. Let us hope we are not there now. Our task is not to eliminate science and technology but rather to direct it, and our social and spiritual efforts as well, to a world more compatible with a "good" life. That "good" life must be one that does not find its sustenance dependent on precious irreplaceable resources which may belong to someone else. It must not be a "good" life which is carried on the backs of others less fortunate than ourselves as has so often been the case in the past.

It is probably an understandable quirk of human nature that as the crisis mounts around us, we find ourselves seeking to punish those to blame for the seemingly separate problems which add up to the total crisis. When gasoline is short and increasingly more expensive, we think of the oil-producing nations as villains because they seek to get as much as they can for their products, just as we have always done. When the price of food goes up we seek to limit the price that farmers

7

---------------------------------------------------------------------------

Of material things what can we have?
We can be warm
We can avoid hunger
We can work with a purpose
We can have a modicum of leisure of our choosing
We can have books
We can have companions
We can have joy
We can have the sun, the moon, the rivers, the rain, the stars,
    and the wind
We are, as we have always been, the husbandmen of this
    earth
We must leave as much as we take
In modest possessions we can have happiness and safety
In opulence, we can have fear and darkness ahead
And we can choose one or the other

---------------------------------------------------------------------------

can get for their goods regardless of what those goods cost to produce. We want all kinds of services from our government, but bitterly oppose the taxes required to pay for those services. Then, of course, we curse the politicians who are forced to try to satisfy our selfish and irrational whims.

We cannot seem to face the fact that for the most part, our troubles are the results of our own collective desires. There are few, if any, long term villains in the mounting problems around us. There are undoubtedly a few persons who take advantage of a stressful situation, but they didn't really cause it, and they don't really affect it much in the long term. The causes, as well as the problems, are serious and deep. They are not solely technological, nor solely economic, nor solely political, nor solely sociological. They are all of these things. Effectively dealing with them will take generations, and in the process our living situation will be profoundly and permanently changed. Whether those changes will be for the better or worse is up to us. Insofar as we continue in the *gimmie gimmie gimmie for free* philosophy peddled by the hawks and hangers on of the so-called consumer movement, our future will be nothing but increasingly bleak and dissappointing— but if we can again develop a spirit in which self-reliance is a virtue, and add to it the realization that we are as responsible to those around us as we are to ourselves, our future could be exceedingly bright, perhaps in the overall better than ever before.

So, what are the values that encourage such a transition to a brave new world—not one of an Aldous Huxley but rather of an Erasmus or a Spinoza?

# GLIMPSES OF THE TRANSITION

Thus, the material and economic transition coming for everyone on this earth is largely unknown and little understood. It will not necessarily come as a cataclysm unless we are foolish enough to pretend it is not there. Rather, it will come over a period of years as the tide comes in—a little at a time, each wave traveling only slightly farther than the last, and sometimes even appearing to recede somewhat before continuing its relentless movement. We have time to prepare, and it is not clear that the new world must be worse than the last—it could even be better if we prepare carefully and work for its coming in a positive and thoughtful way.

But how do we prepare? The "back to nature" movements are probably a precursor of the problems ahead, if not the solutions. Such movements often turn their back on modern technology and seek to prepare in that way. They are sincere, but we are many generations away from nature living. We have all forgotten that nature, while unbelievably beautiful, can be unbelievably cruel as well. We have forgotten that most of our efforts for centuries have been directed towards

11

governing nature's influence over us, not immersing ourselves in it. Nature without science and technology has some lovely gifts at times, but she also gives unchecked disease, famine, drought, and starvation. We cannot prepare for what is to come by simply embracing unbridled nature unless we are prepared to see four-fifths or more of the current world population die, including probably ourselves. Despite all this, we cannot prepare by fighting nature at every turn. The "back to nature" groups have a vital point when they say we must be "in harmony" with nature. Being in harmony does not mean singing the same tune simultaneously, it means singing a different tune simultaneously, but a tune which gives a desirable and pleasing result when sung with the first one. The analogy is indeed subtle, but it is a very good one.

In all probability, we will try to prepare in a patchwork way by attacking each problem individually as it comes up. If we have a medical problem, we can research it until we find a cure. If we are short of food, we will try to develop an even more intensive agriculture. If we are short of energy we will search for new and better sources. We will work very hard to find new and foolproof methods of birth control, and so on.

In fact, we must never abandon such efforts. They are crucial to our material survival which is an absolutely necessary goal. Those of us who are the technicians of life (and we all are really) must make a great effort in pursuit of these goals, either in searching out new material solutions or more intelligently practicing the old ones. We must not join that cult of people who consider the pursuit of such material goals as debasing, perhaps even immoral. While simultaneously condemning such material goals, however, by their very survival they are required to either pursue them or take advantage of their pursuit by others.

And yet, somehow we sense, as do the back to nature people, that material goals are insufficient, and if they represent our sole efforts, they can be totally destructive. Our uncon-

---------------------------------------------------------------------------

It is impossible to help only yourself
It is equally impossible to help others without helping
    yourself

---------------------------------------------------------------------------

nected patchwork efforts can, and often do, counteract one another even though each one appears individually meritorious. To borrow the words of the theoretical mathematician, material goals are necessary and honorable, but by themselves, totally insufficient.

But again, what is missing? What are our true values? Are we not simply people in the sense that we relate to other people? Otherwise we are animals—but how do we relate? We speak glibly about survival, but what is survival after material needs are met, and if there is nothing else, why bother?

Perhaps the next thing we should pursue is personal pleasure in its many forms. Certainly personal pleasure now and then can provide a necessary, welcome, and worthy respite from our daily cares. But we have ages of experience to tell us that those whose situation allows them the continuous pursuit of personal pleasure find in the end that permanent satisfaction is completely elusive, and they generally wind up among the saddest of human beings. Again, it appears that the (occasional) pursuit of pleasure is necessary and desirable, but insufficient.

If not just pleasure, what other values can we pursue which give not just material and bodily survival, but which also make it all worth while? What is it in the human makeup that demands a direction for life extending beyond survival and pleasure? What restlessness leads us to seek these higher values, and what are those values? Can they be arrived at in any logical way? Is there an intellectual approach to a sense of meaningful values about life? Perhaps there is a special form of religion which gives a greater sense of truth than some others. Certainly many different religions claim to be "the one true faith"—or is there only one?

---------------------------------------------------------------------------

Just because we believe that we belong exclusively to God
doesn't mean that He belongs exclusively to us

---------------------------------------------------------------------------

# ON SINCERITY

Let us search out some of the things we might think are connected with values and examine them. Perhaps we can begin with the word *Sincerity*. Many of us, at one time or another, have become sincerely interested in a cause of some kind. It may be evangelism in our religion; it may be the promotion of education; it may be national patriotism; or it may be in the promotion of justice for one group or another. Perhaps it is in the pursuit of some environmental goal such as clean air or wilderness preservation. There are uncountable causes. Most of them are probably necessary and worthwhile, and it is absolutely vital that we give them our sincere support. We all need causes to satisfy our psyche.

But isolated sincerity has its problems. When we evangelize our religion we sometimes assume that all others are wrong or at least inferior. When we sincerely promote national patriotism we may be doing well, but just such sincere promotion of national patriotism in some countries has resulted in genocide for millions of people in this century alone. History is replete with waves of terrorism that occasionally swept (and still sweep) the world, all perpetrated in the name of faith, or justice, or national patriotism, and for an impeccably rightous cause—often by highly literate and certainly the world's most *sincere* people. And yet if we have no causes, no belief beyond ourselves, we are the most miserable of human beings.

Clearly sincerity, like a multitude of other things, can be the tool of both good and evil. Sincerity, to be good, must be coupled with carefully chosen values and thus it too is necessary, but insufficient by itself.

---------------------------------------------------------------------------

We do not become evil deliberately
We become evil unintentionally
By processes of rationalization so slow that we are unaware of
    them
No man ever lived who in his own mind thought of himself as
    evil
He may have been fair in his own mind
He may have been practical in his own mind
He may have been realistic in his own mind
He may have been giving judgement in his own mind
He may have been faithful to his cause in his own mind
He may even have been moral in his own mind
And all of the murders, and thievery, and wars, and infan-
    ticides, and genocides, and tortures, and slavery, and ter-
    rorism in history have been perpetrated by such fair,
    practical, realistic, judging, faithful, and moral men and
    women (in their own minds)
And that is why God's forgiveness is for all, including them

---------------------------------------------------------------------------

# ON INTELLECTUALISM AND
# THE UNIVERSITIES

Let us next examine intellectualism. Many would say that the pursuit of knowledge is the most honorable and useful of all of life's endeavors. But knowledge of what and for what? Some believe that science, technology, medicine, etc., can contribute most to the good of mankind. Others say, however, that such pursuits are pedestrian and that true intellectualism lies in the liberal arts—in literature, music, philosophy, and art—witness that some of life's greatest pleasures come from these. Still others would say that no one is truly educated until he has become thoroughly knowledgeable in both endeavors. Clearly, intellectuals themselves have severe disagreements on their favorite word. Perhaps there is no such thing as a truly educated human being, there being only various degrees of ignorance in different things.

We shall leave to wiser beings (with idle time on their hands) the resolution of this centuries-old debate, but we will assume the audacity to make some observations about intellectual pursuits in general.

Certainly the pursuit of the sciences and their resulting technologies have contributed much to the material well-being of much of the human race. We assume their pursuit is honorable and their contributions will continue. Indeed we could not survive without them. At the same time, it must be said that these pursuits provide tools to be used by mankind, and these tools have been used for both good and evil. A famous philosopher once observed that technology is neither good nor evil, it is strictly neutral.

It is not at all clear, however, that the artists, writers, and philosophers have any more golden route to life's full meaning than do the scientists and technologists, nor for that matter than the untutored woodchopper. The philosophical approach gives us a Spinoza but it also gives a Machiavelli. Artists of all kinds reflect life as they see it, but their craft is equally apt to express the pathos of life as well as the joy of it—and of course they should—because life has pathos and joy, and the great artists of the world have simply kept that fact before us.

The great men of philosophical ideas have similarly presented us with a variety of life value situations, but there is in philosophy no clear siren call to the correct ones for us to follow. Indeed it is completely unreasonable to expect that there could be such a clear guide in philosophy.

The educational and intellectual pursuits of all kinds can certainly be broadening, contributory, and worth while, but their message on a sense of values is clouded at best (though magnificent clues may crop up here and there).

Further, intellectual pursuit to the exclusion of all others often has a somewhat seamy side. There is a special form of snobbishness among some who consider themselves intellectual, and that very snobbishness blinds them to the reality and totality of the whole earth, including the very supporting ground on which they stand.

Indeed, the French royal court at the time of the French revolution was an intellectual one, but its blindness to its surroundings was so severe that the whole of France rose up against it. This was not just because it was intellectual, of course, but certainly its intellectualism in the last analysis

22

should have helped it prevent, or at least moderate, the holocaust that was the French revolution.

We must note that throughout history, governments run by pure intellectuals have generally been dismal failures—as have governments that have ignored what their intellectuals told them.

Intellectualism is a two-edged sword. At its best it is one of the greatest tools of modern man (yes—philosophy and art are tools for good and evil just as are science and technology).

At its worst, intellectualism degenerates to self worship and the pursuit of certification by means of university degrees. A degree should merely indicate that a person has finished a program of study (and perhaps research) and therefore has achieved some measure of competence in a few groups of subjects. It does not give that person a special edge in creativity or a corner on all knowledge. Indeed it sometimes seems to suppress creativity. A doctoral dissertation is seldom that work of original creation which university faculties solemnly vow that it must be, and after their awarding, degrees are often displayed by their holders like a peacock displays his tail feathers, and with approximately the same honor and distinction.

An illustration of another aberration which has grown out of the house of pseudo-intellectualism is our worship of the university student, and worse, yet, his worship of himself. A world famous diplomat once rightly said—"The issue is not what the student is, he is nothing yet. The issue is what he might become in future years if his intellectual pursuit is diligent and his values are carefully chosen."

It is interesting to observe many students in their devotion to causes of various kinds. University students (probably fortunately) will always be involved in causes because they are young, dedicated, sincere (!), full of energy that needs an outlet, and completely unencumbered by experience (and

23

---------------------------------------------------------------

There is no thespian so talented
No scientist or professor so brilliant
No lawyer so clever
No official so great
In short, no person so important
    that he can place himself above
    moral responsibility in his
    relationship to fellow humans

---------------------------------------------------------------

often unencumbered by logic either). They are often a catalyst for needed social change. But sometimes many of them become the programmed robots of clever dialecticians and slogan mongers—never seeking the origins or deeper meaning of the words they shout in choral unison.

Our failing in education for those students has not been in teaching them which causes are right and which are wrong. We are not wise enough for that. Our failing has been our inability to teach them to probe deeply into the origins and real purposes of the cause they espouse—to examine its values if you will. In short, we fail to teach them to use the so-called critical intellectual approach we are supposed to be instilling in them, but which we so seldom use ourselves.

Critical intellectual analysis is one of the greatest tools available to modern civilization. And yet, intellectualism alone cannot provide the values we seek. Intellectualism, like all the rest, is necessary but insufficient.

No person achieves true respect from others
    by virtue of office or degrees alone
Subservience and courtesy perhaps
But whether behind those subservient and courteous eyes lies
    true respect or ridicule or hatred has nothing to do with
    the title,
    but everything to do with the title holder

# ON ECONOMIC AND POLITICAL SYSTEMS

Perhaps we can somehow create an economic system that inherently has the desired values which seem so elusive. We have now had centuries of experience with economic systems espousing capitalism, or socialism, or that confusing (but not necessarily all bad) mixture of the two that so many of us now live in. That experience teaches us that any economic system yet devised by man can either respect the dignity and welfare of individual human beings or unmercifully trample them. Economic systems are amoral, and their quality is determined primarily by the quality of those persons that run them. Economic systems are inevitably intertwined with political systems, of course. Unfortunately, no one person (or small group of persons) has the wisdom to make all the decisions for all the people, so most of the world, if they had a choice, would opt for more or less free economic systems and democratic political systems. But even therein lies a problem. If that group of economically free men and women who opt for democracy do not individually have at least some of the values we seek, they will soon lose their economic and political freedom. Freedom and individual responsibility are synonymous, and that restriction applies to the highest government official as well as the least influential citizen.

But what is individual responsibility? Is it going along quietly with the government or crowd? Often it is, but sometimes that is precisely the antithesis of the individual responsibility necessary for freedom. How do we know which to do? It is easy to know, of course—our sense of values tells us—but what values? It appears that economic and political systems, while obviously necessary, are also woefully insufficient by themselves.

# ON THE MEDIA

Perhaps we can learn of the values we seek through the efforts of our great newspapers and radio and television stations—that is, the media, as we call it.

This enormous force in our society sees as its foundation the long-standing tradition (and Constitutional Amendment) giving the right of free speech. To this extent, the media sees clearly indeed. It fights, at every turn, attempts that it sees, or thinks it sees, to make its voice more restrictive, and again, well it should. Columnists, editors, and commentators are replete with reasons why the media should never be required to reveal its sources, or should be permitted to print anything regardless of fact or damage done thereby.

It has been unquestionably true throughout history everywhere, that when a despot wishes to absolutely control a government, he must somehow muzzle the media. Thus freedom of the media is fundamental to a free society and we must forever guard it.

However, we should not worship it, for like intellectualism and law, it is a priceless asset but a poor diety. Too often parts of the media, like some parts of the legal profession, come to regard themselves as the final judge and jury for all mankind. Suggestions that it might well exercise some responsibility and respect towards the freedom, dignity, and privacy of others are often met with vituperation and senseless attacks designed to mask the media's obvious failings. A media attack on a president, or on anyone else, can be as despotic, cruel, and nationally destructive as anything imaginable, and if it continues, just as dangerous to our freedoms. Too often, the media's tools include ridicule, rumor-mongering, guilt by association, half truths, and rampant speculation without any accompanying real investigation or analysis. Different branches of the media pick up each other's rumors and splash them for psychological effect rather than fundamental truth. This is not just true of the yellow tabloids but sometimes of major newspapers and networks as well.

The media, in pursuit of its own precious freedom, is sometimes quite willing to forget the real historical meaning of freedom of the press and freedom of speech. The rights of freedom of the press and free speech were originally intended to mean the right of the people to be informed on all sides of all major issues. It does not and never did mean a license to malign, scandalize, and ridicule with little (or perhaps without any) solid evidence.

One responsibility of the media includes informing the public of the things it needs to know, and indeed we should be eternally grateful that such a responsibility is taken seriously. Other responsibilities include avoiding editorial ego trips, superficial analysis, ridicule of every new idea, or destruction of public figures with flimsy, or perhaps even a complete lack, of evidence. Too often, these responsibilities are ignored. To be fair, equally often they are taken very seriously by many people in the media. It is unquestionably true that the media has exposed and helped eliminate much that has been bad in our government, but it is also true that it has willfully contributed to the destruction of much that is good. We dare not pass laws defining the limits of the media because no one is wise enough to write them. Clearly the media, like the rest of us, desperately needs a better set of values, whatever they might be. The verdict, as before—necessary but insufficient.

# ON INSTITUTIONS

If not economic and political systems, how about our great institutions—our universities, churches, great corporations, foundations, unions, governments, perhaps even the United Nations—maybe they can provide the values and salvation we seek. They have seemingly provided a steady direction in the past—sometimes a mission, sometimes a shelter within which to worship, work or play. Any student of history can see without difficulty that institutions are clearly an essential part of any worthwhile lasting civilization.

But institutions are not immortal merely because they were once good. They often forget the mission which led to their foundation and become self-serving only to those within—forgetting that major support which keeps them viable generally comes from without. They become havens for their own bureaucrats, whether those bureaucrats are government or company officials, or clergymen, or university presidents or vice presidents, or deans, or professors, or international representatives, or whatever. A sure sign of a decaying institution is one which consumes most of its resources for the sustenance of its own internal workings rather than for its assigned or chosen mission. Such institutions resist all change, particularly if that change calls for a reworking and streamlining of those internal workings which are all consuming. The longevity of an institution really hinges on whether those that support it from without truly believe in the values the institution promulgates or whether those supporters believe the institution actually promulgates the values it says it does.

When institutions begin to fall, the chaos created is often very great, and that chaos does not cease until some new institutions arise and until the surviving old ones become sufficiently renewed so that they can deal with the new order of events. The chaos does not die down until those new institutions promulgate to the majority of the populace around them values and actions which inspire confidence. It is not automatically true that the new stability giving values and actions, once achieved, are better than the old ones. They may be worse. History is full of such cases.

Thus our faith in our institutions must go deeper than just having them be clubs, or unions, or churches, or social groups, or economic units, and the like. That faith and confidence must be built on the values that undergird those institutions. Institutions, like all else it seems, are necessary but insufficient.

# ON THE FAMILY

Before leaving institutions, it is worthwhile to single out one that is very special and perhaps the most sacred—the family. It is our common expectation that the family should pass on the values of importance to its offspring, and so it should.

Much has been written in recent years on the decline of the family, and we hear such phrases as "the extended family," "the broken family," "the communal family," and so on. Do we expect each of these to pass on the same values? Certainly the values of one are sometimes incompatible with another; and who is to say when one is good and the other bad? Families are made of people, and people cannot pass on values they do not possess.

There is, however, one fact that many find comforting. Families may be reinterpreted, or broken, or may have imperfect values, or be destroyed by situations out of their control. But the family concept is the one institution that will survive as long as humankind survives. It was the first institution and it will be the last. We are indeed people only in the sense of our relationship to other people. A life alone, totally unconnected with other people, is a meaningless life, and the primordial urge to relate to and love those close to us is genetically ingrained in life itself. It cannot be permanently eliminated by any power of man whatever.

-------------------------------------------------------------------------------

My mother and father were not perfect—as none of us are
  perfect
But they did love their children and they loved each other,
  and
    that issue was never in doubt at any time in our lives
And I now realize as an older man, that for those reasons, I
  must
    consider myself among the world's very privileged
    human beings

-------------------------------------------------------------------------------

# ON PEOPLE

In a real sense, everything we have been critically discussing represents an institution of some sort or other. The legal system and the media are institutions just as are churches, unions, some corporations, and families.

Before criticism becomes too harsh, we must remember that institutions are not buildings or organization charts. They are people. From their formative stages, throughout their rise, fall, and final destruction they are still people, and only people. Further, their successes and failures are finally decided by people, both within the institution and those outside who are most affected by it. When parts of the media exploit sensationalism to the detriment of our culture, they would fail miserably in the attempt if part of that culture did not respond as Pavlovian dogs. An unscrupulous attorney who seeks to create litigation for personal gain only with no concern for fairness or justice would have no base on which to stand if he did not have a greedy client to participate in the action. Similar statements can be made of every institution and profession. Those of us who stand outside and do not participate have failed as much as those within. Any idealistic social structure, no matter how carefully designed to preserve freedom and dignity of the individual, will fail if those on whom it is built do not respect and maintain its ideals in their

41

deeds, not just their words. Thus our critical comments, if they are to be fair, must be directed towards people and specifics, not towards whole institutions or professions.

The moral mood of humanity shifts like the sands of the desert, and just as we begin to think it is in its rightful place, it has drifted away. In truth, we perhaps cannot have it any other way. The mood and direction of humanity must be flexible or it would shatter on every incoming wave.

To survive the coming economic and social dislocation of which we speak will require such flexibility on our part. Survival will not be possible if we have a shoddy set of basic human values, and yet choosing those values is perhaps the most difficult problem of all. We must do it with extreme care.

# ON RELIGIOUS FAITH

And if all that has gone before is insufficient, how about religious faith? Can we find a true answer to a sense of values in our God? Can we simply leave everything to Him, or does He even exist? Is there a grand design for all things, a pre-destination or fate for the world, or do we have a responsible and meaningful role to play—and does the outcome in part depend on us?

These questions are not new, they are all millenniums old. The best minds of antiquity have grappled with them, and have arrived at conclusions as diverse as the stars. How can those of us whose minds are much simpler arrive at meaningful directions and purposes for ourselves? Has there ever been a mature human being on earth who has not at some time in the privacy of his own mind grappled with these greatest of all questions?

For those at the stage of life where these questions are important (that stage can occur anywhere from age ten to ninety and over and over again in between), there are a number of ready-made solutions offered up for us to consider.

The first thing we might consider is to not believe in any power higher than ourselves, and that even our very existence came about by the merest chance.

It may be that intellectual efforts alone cannot give us a

complete set of values to live by, but it is difficult to sustain (on intellectual grounds) an atheistic belief in creation by total chance. The first thing learned by a student of biology, physics, chemistry, or any other science is that the world seems to be governed by a rather well-defined and ordered set of natural rules. Generally, these rules are dependable and experiments to examine them give repeatable results if those experiments are well-designed and executed. Laws of physics, once discovered, tend to last for a long time, in some cases forever in the domain of reference in which they were discovered. They are sometimes expanded, or limited to certain conditions, or found to be replaced by other laws in new domains of reference, but they seldom are eliminated. Further, physical laws tend to interact with and be consistent with one another. Indeed, research in science is often as not concentrated in areas where things seem to be inconsistent. The purpose of that research is generally to find an elusive consistency which is believed (almost by childlike faith) to be there somewhere. Sooner or later, it is often found.

At the very least, the universe is governed by consistent interacting laws. To believe that all occurred by the merest chance is to believe that when a basket of coins is dumped out, they will all land and remain on edge. Thus again it is intellectually difficult to accept a position of total athiesm, remembering the pitfalls of pure intellectualism in the first place.

Yet before we ridicule this position of atheism, let us not forget that some very able men in history (Marx and Freud for example) claimed to be atheists, and one of the most powerful governments of the world today claims it as a foundation pillar.

It might be well to remember that both Marx and Freud were dedicated to opposing what they saw as an oppressive and merciless church holding its people in bondage through fear and mysticism. We may or may not believe that their

44

---

Scholarly studies of Biblical history
Militant cries of powerful men
Rigid views of the fundamentalist preacher
None of these can bring me to God
But the still quiet of a summer night
A walk alone and yet with God
A walk with no earthly purpose
The bathing and cleansing of one's faith in the quietness of
    love
In these does one begin to understand that faith and knowl-
    edge have power
But the most important of these is faith—faith in God's love

---

view of the church was valid or fair, but there is no doubt that it was completely sincere (!).

Can a good man or woman be an atheist? Of course they can. Major humanitarian contributions have been made by such people—but whatever purpose of life they have must be created by themselves. Thus there can be no greater divine power for that person above himself. That would seem to be, at best, a very lonely role to play in this universe, but that fact still gives us no excuse to deprecate his integrity or values.

It might seem that the more valid question from an intellectual point of view really is—if the universe is so well and consistently organized from a scientific point of view, who or what organized it and for what purpose if any? This is the starting place of the agnostic. As an agnostic, one can believe on intellectual grounds that there probably is a higher order of things. However we simply do not know how or why. More important, we don't know what the purpose of our own existence is in the overall scheme of things, or even if there is any special purpose for us. In this state we probably have built our intellectual pillar as high as it can go.

To jump from agnosticism to a strong faith in a divine power that cares for us requires something more than intellect. It requires what the name implies, an act of faith. We might call it blind faith, particularly if we have found no way to make the jump.

But is it blind? Is it even necessarily anti-intellectual? Anti-intellectualism would be to believe something for which there is adequate evidence that what we believe is not true.

Our intellectualism tells us of at least some of the order—of the existence of a grand design—of the great consistency of much of what is and what happens on the earth and in the heavens. It does not tell us if we, as individuals, and those we love, are viewed by the *grand designer* as of individual worth, to be nurtured, encouraged, and eternally preserved by some method or in some form unknown to any of us. Conversely, it does not tell us if we are all mere toy soldiers to be lined up and then swept down to dust. Our intellectualism does not explain the mass destruction of human life in war, famine, pestilence, or disease, and our intellectualism does not explain the "peace that passeth all understanding" that some fortunate individuals achieve. It provides no proof or disproof in such matters. That is why the agnostic position (that is, we simply don't know) is as far as intellectualism can take us. Therefore we must pursue these most difficult of questions through some other route.

All of the religions of the world must somehow deal with the step from intellectual agnosticism to faith. After all, the least educated jungle savage as well as the trained scientist is able to intellectually observe, and has observed, the order around him. Night follows day; season follows season, and comes around again; loved ones are born, live, and die. All humans have a sense of their position in their surroundings, it's just that the surroundings are different for different people.

Indeed, many, perhaps thousands, of interpretations of the world's scheme of things have been devised. Every primitive tribe had one or more dieties to worship—the sun, rain, wind, stars, volcanos, rocks, trees, hand-made images—all have served as Gods at one time or another. Some were evangelistic, some were exclusive, some were harsh, some were kind, some were simple and beautiful. An American Indian in the last century was asked his belief about God and he said "I see the sun, the mountains, the stars, I feel the rain and hear the wind, and it is enough."

Some religions, through their prophets, their evangelists, and sometimes through their wars, captured major segments of the earth's population, Christianity, Islam, and Buddhism being prime examples. Each requires the basic act of faith from the true believers. Each has its sacred documents and rituals to assist in keeping the faith pure. Each has its noble principles, and many of those principles are common among them.

But in our western world, where Christianity is dominant, there are thousands of subtle variations. There are churches which use rich liturgy and that seems to help some of the faithful. There are some with rigid dogma to keep the faithful from straying. Others use the rewards of heaven or the fear of hell, fire, and eternal damnation. The signals from organized Christianity are confused. Further, some say there is no salvation (that is—eternal life in harmony with the creator) except through acceptance by grace in a special way. Perhaps so, but what of our many magnificent friends in Islam with a rich literature and belief of their own, and of Judaism which gave so much of the basic faith of both Islam and Christianity, and of the hundreds of millions of followers of Buddha and the teacher Sri Krishna? Are these all eternally rejected because they have not with sincerity (!) repeated the right words in the correctly ordered way?

Perhaps we ourselves might even believe in the eternal forgiveness of the Lord through Jesus Christ (as the words go) but the very words make it impossible for us to then believe that vengeance will then be vested on all the rest who seek the same God, and the same step of faith, by other means. Something in Christ's words tells us that all human beings (yes, all of them) have a dignity that is neither enhanced nor decreased by the recitation of a specific set of words or the practicing of a special dogma. Thus, to those who have found their faith by being born again, or by any of the other methods, we can only express our most heartfelt congratulations and our genuine admiration for their achievement. But we do ask that they tolerate those of us who seek to find our step of faith in some additional way.

But what way? Is there yet another way that we can see the works of a divine creator and thus truly become one of the faithful?

--------------------------------------------------------------------------

I believe in God because I see a rose, one needs nothing else
I believe in Christ because when things are very quiet
    I know that he is near
Although I am a stumbling fool, I am nevertheless God's
    servant, though
    admittedly a poor one
When I fall, and I do often, each time he quietly reprimands
    me
Much the same as we quietly reprimand a little child who is
    not old
    enough to understand the reason
Following the reprimand, he gently comforts us if we but ask
    him to do so
Is this the blind faith so many think it is?
It is faith but it is not blind

--------------------------------------------------------------------------

---------------------------------------------------------------

One of the privileges God gives some of us is to see and know
    personally, and have warm friends among some of His
    servants from His other great religions—Islam, Judaism,
    Hinduism, and others, in their home setting
One cannot observe their devotion to God and their service
    to their fellow man, and still believe that God requires
    them to acknowledge Him in just one way, or through
    one savior to make their servitude valid
How do I know this?—I know because in those quiet moments
    of personal meditation with my personal savior Jesus
    Christ, He tells me so

---------------------------------------------------------------

# ON VALUES AND THOSE WHO HAVE THEM

Perhaps we can see that work of the creator in individual members of one of his greatest achievements: the human race. But we shall not confine our search to holy and pious men—we shall not exclude them, but they will not be the ground of our main search. Neither will we seek to find the work of the creative power solely in those who profess loudly to have found the way (although we won't ignore them either). We will also seek it in some persons who may not have much to say about it at all. We may well even find part of what we seek in persons who themselves have not made the sought-after leap of faith.

Since we cannot find all the values we seek in intellectual or religious pursuits (although we may find some) we will also seek them by observing those who seem to have individual values of great merit. In many cases (perhaps most) we will discover the values we seek in persons who never in their lives have expressed them in words—and thus the job of detection is fascinating as well as rewarding.

As we think about it, we have all known people who (it seemed to us in our hearts) had them. Who are they? One thing is for sure. They, like us, are not perfect. They have suffered, and sinned, and wept, and laughed, and overcome. No one can be hammered on the anvil of life and be without scars. But somehow on these people the scars look more like badges—past mistakes turned to wisdom grown of experience. Not all of us become wiser and more humane because of our experiences, but they did. Their broken bodies and windswept spirits finally become the anchor posts from which each of us can grasp some stability in our own storm-tossed lives. Who are these gentle giants of our kind? Perhaps there could be a little of them in each of us. It is their sense of values we seek to find and emulate.

They come from no special church or faith, perhaps from none at all, and yet perhaps all faiths all over the world have contributed some of them.

They have no minimum or maximum level of formal education. They may be illiterate or men and women of letters.

They have no minimum or maximum status level in our artificially stratified society. They may be famous or unknown to all but a few. If they are famous, more often than not, their fame is for something far removed from the qualities we seek and admire in them.

They may be policemen, or military (as the Centurion of Matthew) or they may be pacifists and concientious objectors, or they may be like many of us, in the troubled in-between.

"They" may be a beloved teacher, but not because of the particular subject taught.

They come from no special profession—they may be sales-

----------------------------------------------------------------------

Do not hesitate to set your life to solving the world's
   problems
For that work is part of your salvation
But do not be so foolish as to think that in your lifetime many
   of them will be solved
What then is a successful life?
If at its end you can look back and truly say that the world is
   a smattering better off because you were here
Then your life will have been successful almost beyond com-
   prehension

----------------------------------------------------------------------

men, plumbers, scientists, janitors, physicians, historians, lawyers, farmers, engineers, bankers, or they may be unemployed or unemployable.

They may be healthy or sick, psychologically sound or mentally ill, free or in prison, and of any race whatever.

They may be silent or talkative, large or small—they may be any of us. Yet, each of them has one or more noble values that partly govern their lives. These values are often unexpressible in their own words, and even they may not be consciously aware of them. None of them have all of these values, but all have some of them. Noble values do not imply sainthood. They are not saints.

They may speak their language with a silver tongue, or their vocabulary may be limited and partly profane.

But they are honest, with themselves and with others.

They have a quiet belief based on experience and observation of the existence of a natural order and a higher power. They have a continual need to ask guidance from that higher power and to respect others doing the same. In the same manner, they have a quiet caution about the messages they believe they receive, and they respect others who seem to receive different messages.

They have a deep reverence for all human life.

They have a deep humility and recognize that they are abysmally ignorant about the universe.

They accept responsibility and take action when it seems that such action can be for a common good. They know that in the end, material benefits for the majority of us must be brought about by services rendered, value for value.

They pursue their ideas with vigor, but always recognize they could be wrong. They do not hesitate to change their ideas and directions when they begin to miss the mark, and they do not concern themselves with the embarrassment of changing or having been wrong.

They recognize that all human beings have strengths and weaknesses. They admire and encourage the strengths of others, but are not particularly critical of the weakness they see in those around them, for they know of their own weaknesses.

They have an absolute abhorrence of arrogance in anyone, and the words vengeance and revenge are not in their vocabulary. They are able to think of no person as their enemy, especially those who consider them an enemy.

They know that ridicule and sarcasm directed towards others is a special form of cruelty, and more often than not it is based on the ignorance of the ridiculer rather than the ridiculed.

---------------------------------------------------------------

What we are is a composite of a few pillars in our back-
　　ground
A teacher here; a friend there; perhaps our parents; perhaps
　　a minister; perhaps an untutored but worldly wise,
　　rough, tough, secretly compassionate woodsman; and a
　　few others God has allowed to deeply touch our lives.
The total influence on us of thousands of others in this world
　　is minuscule compared to any one of those few to whom
　　we owe everything of what we are

---------------------------------------------------------------

They admire achievement and the successful life in others—which is to say the quietly carrying out of chosen tasks. They are able to suppress the natural jealousy we develop for others who seem to succeed more than we do, and they help that person succeed even further.

They are moderate in all things, not falsely modest, and not overbearing, but move smoothly and quietly among their fellow human beings.

They look on life cheerfully, not somberly. They love humor, and are able to laugh most heartily at the funniest of all people—themselves. They do not take themselves too seriously. They know one is not required to wear a hair shirt to serve God.

They have a certain quiet earthiness, subtle but not vulgar, gentle, common, loving but not crude.

They have much self-respect, and therefore respect for all others, and they serve others with neither arrogance nor subservience.

When leadership is required of them, they provide leadership. When leadership is vested in others, they assist that person in achieving successful leadership if they can possibly do so in good conscience. A special sense of values is not necessarily a part of our recognized leaders, nor is it denied a person because he is a leader.

When I ridicule another human being
I turn a person I want as a friend into
    a hurt, resentful enemy
Ridicule does not help a person agree with me
It merely aids that person to despise me
And if I degenerate to ridicule, I deserve those
    feelings of resentment from without
When I am in verbal contact with another, that person
    is either a potential enemy or a potential friend
God spare me from ridicule—not when it is applied to
    me for then I have begun to overcome
Rather spare me from temptation to use it, for then
    I am surely morally defeated

They recognize the need to devote part of their lives to causes, but they do not use those causes to escape from reality. They can continually examine their own favorite causes with a critical eye.

They know that love is the greatest word in the world—but to really love means to act responsibly to others. They respond to the word love in all of its meanings, and they know that all of the meanings are intertwined.

They respect the honor of work and the dignity of workers—all work and all workers doing all tasks.

They understand the need to carry out the tasks for our time, and they put their shoulder to the wheel most appropriate for them.

They think of pious behavior in others (as well as themselves) not as a sin, but merely as an outwardly obvious weakness for all to see.

They guard the earth with extreme care and respect it always—never allowing it to be permanently damaged, but recognizing that it must of necessity slowly and continually change.

They accept that we cannot fully know of the creator's ultimate objective for us—but they know there is one and they trust in the infinite wisdom of that creator.

They accept that adversity, disappointment, and sorrow will be part of the life of everyone, and they strive to help themselves and others overcome it.

They find their special method of prayer, whatever it is, as their means of communication with the infinite, and they practice it without being so foolish as to think theirs is the only way.

They know that all humans are imperfect, and while they regret their mistakes and try not to repeat them, they do not become incapacitated by feelings of guilt or self pity.

They know and love the joy of music, and art, and literature.

They are dedicated to the preservation of the natural beauty of nature in places here and there, so that their children may know of it, and of the earth's past.

They love justice, and know that it must be administered with extreme care, for justice in the eyes of one is often injustice in the eyes of another. They know that if justice is poorly applied, then it simply creates injustice for others, which calls for more justice, which creates more injustice, and in the end, injustice is applied to all. They know that justice must look forward, not just backward, and be applied to all people equally—it must not be a mechanism of making the children pay for the past sins of their fathers.

They are curious about the universe—how it works, what it is made of, what others think about it—and they encourage and admire intellectual curiousity in others, and they know that such admirable characteristics can be found in anybody, not just the formally educated.

They do not fear to look for truth, and when they find it, they are not afraid or ashamed to alter things to accommodate that truth.

They truly believe in allowing everyone to speak his mind without fear of reprisal, and they guard that right for everyone, for that may be the only way we can learn of needed new directions, or learn of our past mistakes.

They accept the spiritual and material responsibility for themselves and for their families, and they teach their children to do the same. They guard their childen until they can care for themselves. Then they cease guarding and rejoice—but they love them always, no matter what happens.

The list is not complete—it goes on and on. You may add those values you have observed from those very few who have, by their influence, made you what you are. You really know, if you think about it, that your judgment on any event or any observation is largely determined by your personal set of values. Altruism, paranoia, hypocrisy, humility, joy, sadness—all human reactions are influenced by our set of values, and in part are simply reflections of what we really are.

Without a set of values, we are spiritually naked. We can

interpret anything as anything and really believe it. Genuine altruism is interpreted as cunning trickery, and all sorts of dire motives are sometimes derived from the most innocent of remarks and actions. These paranoid characteristics can infect groups of people, even nations, as well as individuals, and the hatreds engendered can last for tens of generations. We can see much of this on both sides of many of today's world conflicts.

-------------------------------------------------------------------

It is true that sometimes nothing can be so self-renewing as
the occasional moments we have alone (and sometimes
with God)
But that self-renewal exhibits its value only in later interac-
tions with other people.

-------------------------------------------------------------------

# IN PREPARATION FOR TOMORROW

So now, as we face this material transition and the future sometimes looks unknown and dark, let us realize that the crisis is, first, one of a sense of values, and secondly, one of material well-being. Thus we first need to prepare our spirits by trying to be at least a little bit like those quiet and gentle giants that are really all around us.

Next let us recognize that if each of us can develop such a set of values, then the structures, and governments, and institutions which pyramid upon us will reflect those values, and then we can turn our hand to the best medicine, the best agriculture, the best science and technology, the best ecology, the best literature, the best philosophy, the best theology, the best peace making, the best governing, the best justice, and the best institutions that the creator's guidance and the needs of the times can lead us to produce. That is how we can prepare for what is coming.

And let us acknowledge that all of the great human contributions have been made by quite imperfect human beings. Perfection in humans is undefinable, unreachable, and probably even undesirable.

Thus we can acknowledge that our activities and directions may have to change from time to time. Despite our best intentions, we will occasionally be wrong. The future for us (as it has always been for all mankind) is like a maze. No single direction will get us through, but a constant change of direction plus correction of our inevitable mistakes probably can.

What should not change is our sense of human values, because those very values will tell us when our direction becomes wrong, and we can then change that direction without fear, guilt, or shame.

When the next crisis comes and grows and sorely tries us all, and wanes, we will survive.

But it will not be because of the militant, or the pious, or the famous, or because of any special social or political system. It will be because of these people of whom we speak—those who have the sense of values, and the faith, and the drive, and the honesty, and the cleverness (all by the gift of the creator) to see us through. They may well be (as some of us believe) the creator's greatest achievement, and the final proof of his existence.